OUR GOD REIGNS

THE TRIUMPH AND GLORY OF EASTER

A MUSICAL BY

TOM FETTKE

NARRATIONS BY CHIP ARNOLD

LILLENAS
PUBLISHING COMPANY

LILLENAS.COM

OUR GOD REIGNS

OUR GOD REIGNS is designed to be easily and effectively presented no matter what resources are at your disposal. It is flexible enough to be staged simply or more colorfully, with small choir or a larger choir.

Following are a few ideas. Feel free to be creative and adapt **Our God Reigns** to whatever personnel and equipment you have at hand.

PRODUCTION OPTIONS

Option One: Choir & Narrator—The entire musical can be effectively presented with choir and narrator only. The house lights should be dimmed or taken out completely at the beginning of the musical, leaving only the stage area lit. The choir can remain seated or standing in position on stage. The character of the Blind Man could be read as narration by the pastor or a member of the choir or congregation. He should remain on stage beside the choir with a microphone for the monologues. Special lighting on the narrator will enhance the effect of the readings.

Option Two: Blind Man in Character—The Blind Man can be put in character. Let him move about the stage and speak directly to the audience. Either biblical costume and modern dress may be used. A follow-spot might be necessary.

Option Three: Add Visual Effects—In combination with Options One or Two, the musical can be richly enhanced by the use of visual media. A variety of visuals are available, from slides and video centering on Passion Week to projected lyrics. Many scenes would work beautifully if silently projected on a screen or screens behind or above the choir as they perform. You can achieve a similar effect by projecting individual slides of the biblical characters in dramatic scenes. Use them to enhance specific moments in the songs or monologues.

Option Four: Pantomime or Tableau—Have choir members or others silently act out the scenes in the monologues or songs. Use either pantomime (with movement) or tableau (fixed scenes). This will require some measure of staging and rehearsal time.

Set Requirements—There are no specific set requirements. You can use no stage decorations whatsoever, or you can build a fully painted set. If you prefer a middle ground, try artistically draped fabric, an assortment of greenery, and/or colorful banners.

LIGHTING

OUR GOD REIGNS can be presented with general sanctuary lighting.

However, the ability to darken and/or spotlight areas of the stage, and to use follow-spots for individual soloists and the Narrator, will add dramatic focus to the overall production.

You may want to bring up the house lights at times—for example, if congregational participation is used. Lighting during those songs will help the congregation feel a part of what's happening. Otherwise, the house lights should be completely out. (The Choir Director may want to teach those songs to the congregation several weeks ahead of time.)

If slides, overhead projections, and/or video are used, the house needs to be darkened so the images are visible. The house lights should be brought up again during the Pastor's comments and during any invitation he might want to extend.

CONTENTS

I
Opening

With exaltation ♩ = ca. 92

Arranged by Tom Fettke

Choir unison

*"Our God Reigns"

Our God reigns!

6

reigns! _____ Our God reigns!

How love - ly on the moun - tains are the

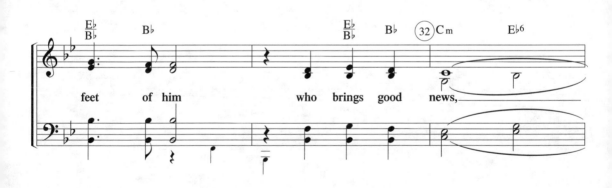

feet of him who brings good news,_____

_____ good news. An - nounc - ing

NARRATOR: The air was choked with dust, the roar of the crowd was deafening. I could barely see Him as He rode the young colt into Jerusalem. Quivering palm branches were everywhere, and waving arms strained to touch Him. Young people danced around Him. Cries of "Hosanna!" echoed above our heads. The excitement rushed through my body like a desert wind, and shouts of praise burst from my lips: "Blessed is the King who comes in the name of the Lord!" I joined hundreds of voices repeating the phrase. Religious leaders insisted Jesus silence His followers, but He replied, "If they keep quiet, the very stones will cry out!" Yes, I thought, let all creation resound with praise! The Hope of the World is now entering Jerusalem in triumph!

II
Hosanna to the King

Arranged by Tom Fettke

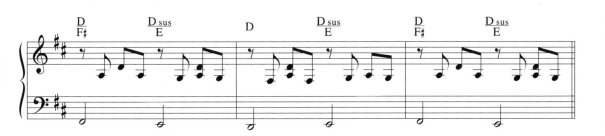

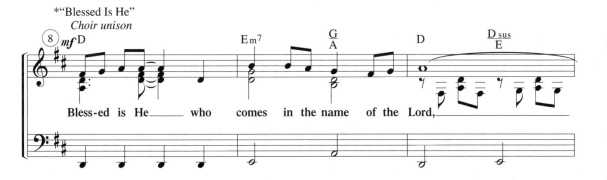

"Blessed Is He"
Choir unison

Bless-ed is He_____ who comes in the name of the Lord,_____

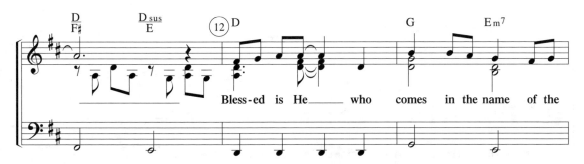

Bless-ed is He_____ who comes in the name of the

14

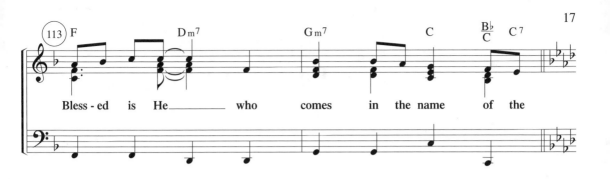

Bless - ed is He _____ who comes in the name of the

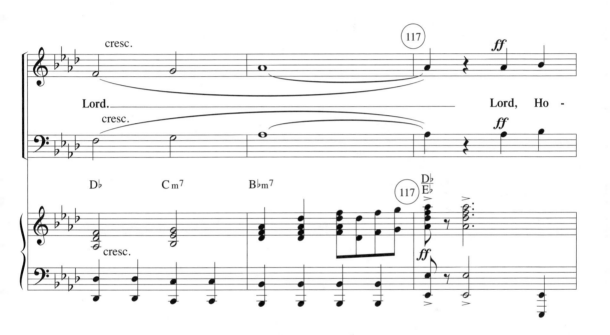

Lord. _____ Lord, Ho -

san - na! _____

III
Jesus–Born to Die

With great expression ♩ = ca. 80

Arranged by Tom Fettke

*"Jesus–Born to Die"
a tempo

Je - sus– born to die; Born to die up-on a tree. Je - sus– born to die; Born to die for you and me.

*"Our God Reigns"

*"Final Moments"

NARRATOR: I could not believe my ears! Some of the same voices that had cried, "Hosanna!" now shouted, "Crucify him!" I also could not believe my eyes. Arms and hands that had waved to greet Him were now clenched, demanding His death. In just a few days the world had turned upside down. I followed Him along the winding road outside the city, His bleeding back straining under the weight of the cross. I stood on the hill of the skull and watched the steel spikes driven through His flesh as a crown of thorns pierced His brow. I listened to the voices, once filled with praise, now hurling insults and curses. How could people turn so quickly on one they had called their king? As I stood beneath the cross and watched the agony of death wrench His body, I heard Him pray, "Father, forgive them. They know not what they do." Only the King of Heaven could have uttered such words of compassion in those final moments.

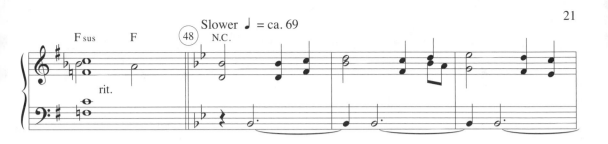

CD: 16

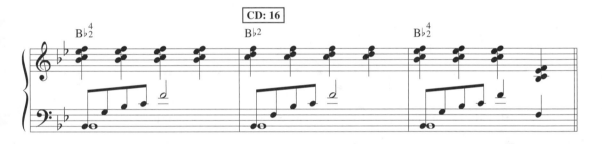

*"The Day He Wore My Crown"

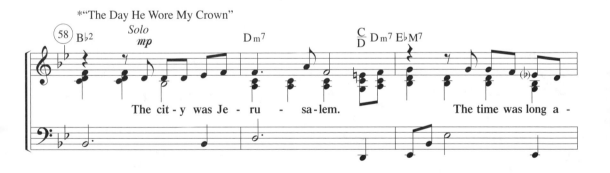

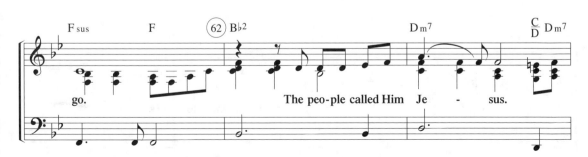

IV
Resurrection Joy

**NARRATOR: Even though Roman soldiers guarded the tomb where Jesus had been buried, some unexplainable force compelled me to remain close by. If He could miraculously change my life and the lives of so many others, couldn't He also come back from the dead? There had been talk of this. Though many wished it to be so, few believed it was possible. I didn't know what I believed. I just knew I was being drawn to this sacred ground. By the third day, several women closely connected to Jesus had come to the tomb to anoint His body. They weren't there more than a minute before they came running back down the path as though they had seen a ghost! Actually, their excitement was the result of angels telling them that Jesus had risen from the dead! Word spread like wild fire! Two of His disciples came to see for themselves, and they also reported an empty tomb. We were overwhelmed! It was as though we had exchanged a lifetime of sadness for pure and unbridled joy.

29

30

32

CD: 25

*"Christ the Lord Is Risen Today"

34

V
Resurrection Hope

Worshipful ♩= ca. 76

Arranged by Tom Fettke

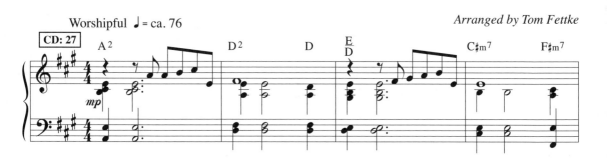

"All Heavens Declares"

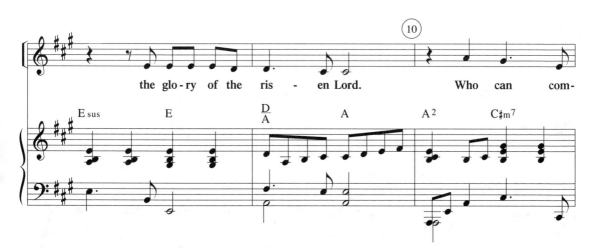

38

CD: 29

*"A Miracle"

Tenderly ♩ = ca. 60

*NARRATOR: I was an eyewitness to the events surrounding Jesus' death and resurrection. If you had asked me about them a few weeks ago, I wouldn't have been able to describe anything to you. You see, I had been blind from birth and destined to live in permanent darkness. Then Jesus came along, spat in the dirt, wiped some mud on my eyes, and told me to wash in the Pool of Siloam. The second I splashed water into my eyes I was stunned by an astonishing, dazzling light, so powerful it knocked me to the ground. In that moment I was given the precious gift of sight. I wanted to see the man who had performed this miracle. But before I could even search for Him, He found me. He asked if I believed in the Son of Man. I said, show Him to me so I may believe. He smiled and said, "You're looking at Him"…I fell down and worshipped Him.

*"He Is Lord"

*"King Jesus"

1st time: Choir unison (large notes)
2nd time: 2 part optional
(Sopranos and Tenors sing small notes)

1. Je-sus is my Lord, my___ Mas-ter and Sav-ior.
2. Je-sus is my King, my___ Shield and De-fend-er.

Je-sus is my Lord, my___ Mas-ter and Sav-ior.
Je-sus is my King, my___ Shield and De-fend-er.

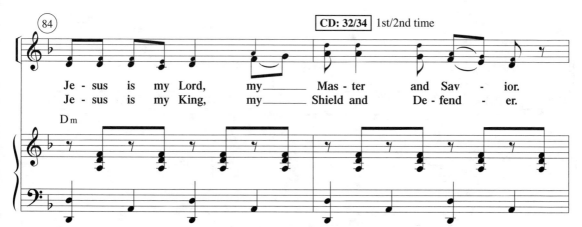

CD: 32/34 1st/2nd time

Je-sus is my Lord, my___ Mas-ter and Sav-ior.
Je-sus is my King, my___ Shield and De-fend-er.

42

Now and for - ev - er - more.
Now and for - ev - er - more.

Pow - er, wis - dom, maj - es - ty Be un - to the____

Lamb._____ Christ is King and Lord of all.

44

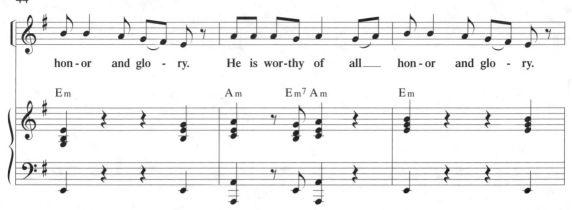

hon-or and glo - ry. He is wor-thy of all__ hon-or and glo - ry.

106

He is wor-thy of all__ hon-or and glo - ry. Now and for-ev - er -

CD: 36

more, hal - le - lu - jah, Now and for - ev - er - more.

VI
Crown Him with Praise

PLEASE NOTE: Copying of this product is NOT covered by CCLI licenses. For CCLI information call 1-800-234-2446.

so, see here His hands, His feet, His side.

Yes, we know, He is a - live.

CD: 39 *"My King"

**Narration begins

**NARRATOR: Jesus healed not only my physical darkness, but my spiritual darkness as well. When He touched me a glorious light filled my life, and the darkness of sin and even death had been conquered. The King I saw riding on a colt that day in Jerusalem is now the mighty King of kings… my King of kings, reigning in heaven forevermore.

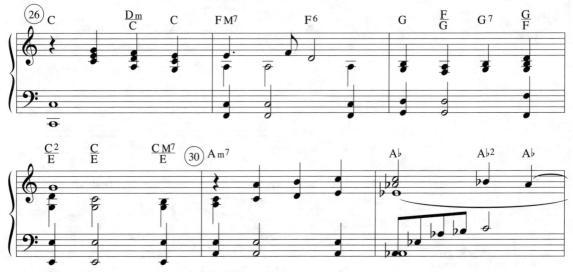

49

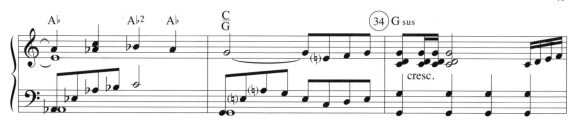

CD: 40

*"Blessing"

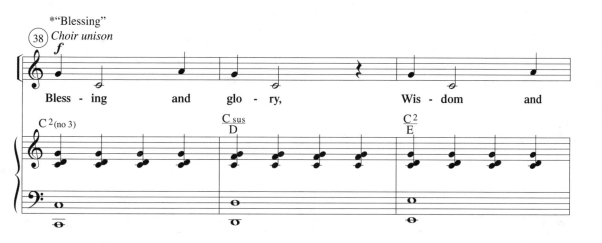

Bless - ing and glo - ry, Wis - dom and

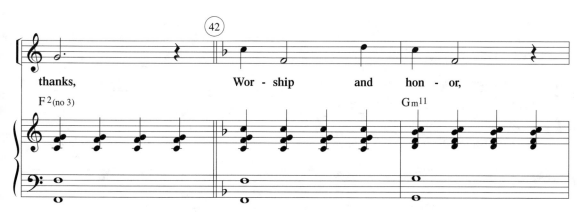

thanks, Wor - ship and hon - or,

*Words by KEN BIBLE, based on Revelation 7:12; Music by TOM FETTKE. Copyright © 2003 by Pilot Point Music (ASCAP) All rights reserved.
Administered by The Copyright Company, 1025 16th Avenue South, Nashville, TN 37212.

50

OUR GOD REIGNS

OUR GOD REIGNS

OUR GOD REIGNS

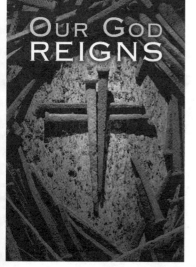

OUR GOD REIGNS

OUR GOD REIGNS

OUR GOD REIGNS

OUR GOD REIGNS

Additional clip art available, in color and black and white, in jpg and tif formats,
on-line at http://www.lillenas.com/clipArt.jsp

CONTENTS